Highlights

Dinosaur Hidden Pictures Puzzles to Highlight

HIGHLIGHTS PRESS

Honesdale, Pennsylvania

wishbone

artist's brush

boomerang

mallet

chef's hat

horseshoe

glove

fork

envelope

swim fin

button

3

envelope

flower

fish

crescent moon

key

lollipop

ice-cream cone

wheel

open book

boot

hammer

carrot

pencil

slice of pizza

toothbrush

banana

basketball

mug

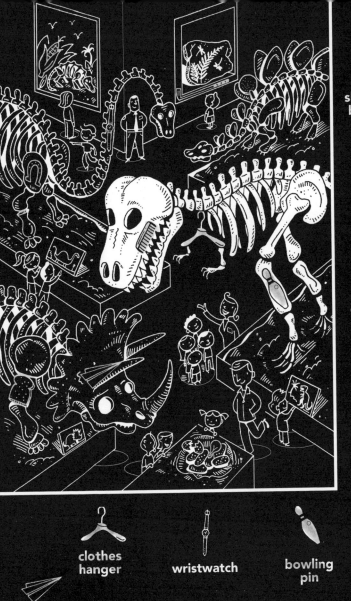

slice of bread

light bulb

ear of corn

comb

vase

clothes hanger

wristwatch

bowling pin

paper airplane

golf club

horseshoe

table-tennis paddle

teacup

flag

mitten

key

comb

slice of bread

duck

toothbrush

crayon

ruler

pencil

book

saltshaker

envelope

spoon

musical note

thimble

comb

feather
duster

toothbrush

tack

mug

spoon

feather

hammer

scissors

zipper

hot dog

slice of bread

fried egg

acorn

fan

crown

slice of
pizza

candle

pear

ladybug

glove

feather

scissors

carrot

peanut

artist's brush

fish

tennis ball

hatchet

barbell

horseshoe

banana

light bulb

pennant

party hat

bowl

shoe

sailboat

ring

heart

sailboat

bowling
ball

sock

domino

baseball
bat

olive

star

candy corn

artist's
brush

needle

toothbrush

teardrop

horseshoe

pen

piece of
popcorn

oar

artist's brush

paper airplane

handbag

kite

noodle

banana

13

fishhook

crown

wedge of
lemon

plunger

flashlight

flyswatter

paper
airplane

spoon

top hat

domino

drinking
straw

toothbrush

diamond

pencil

ladle

teacup ring canoe wedge of lemon carrot

belt envelope ball of yarn ladder lemon mitten

baseball bat

fish

hot dog

slice of
pizza

fishhook

baseball

beehive

crown

candy cane

lightning
bolt

17

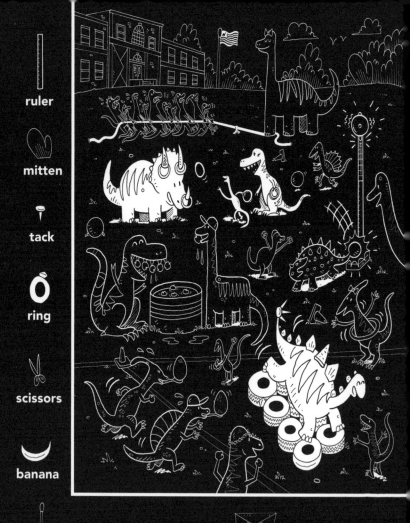

ruler

mitten

tack

ring

scissors

banana

 drumstick

 comb

 envelope

 croissant

 slice of pizza

 boomerang

 slice of bacon

 ice-cream cone

duck

ladder

glove

star

crown

banana

mouse

fishing pole

peacock

fish

megaphone

comb

crescent moon

ruler

drinking straw

chili pepper

roll of tape

shoe

crown

staple

binoculars

saucepan

mallet

mug

flashlight

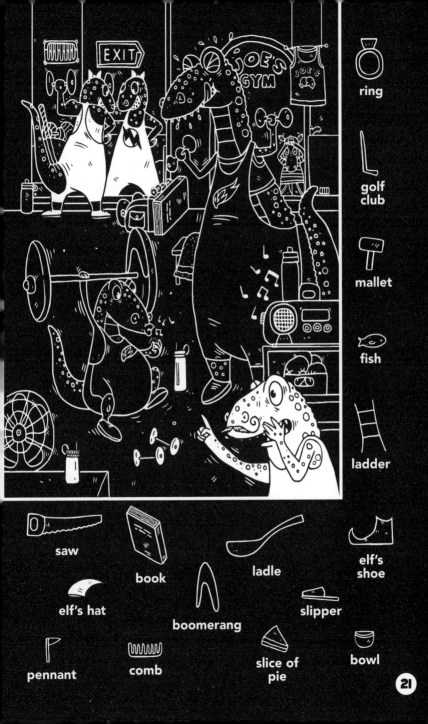

ring

golf club

mallet

fish

ladder

saw

book

ladle

elf's shoe

elf's hat

boomerang

slipper

pennant

comb

slice of pie

bowl

21

banana

needle

ice-cream bar

teapot

heart

slice of bread

artist's brush

fish

paintbrush

22

high-heeled shoe

pencil

lemon

sock

open book

spoon

slice of pie

23

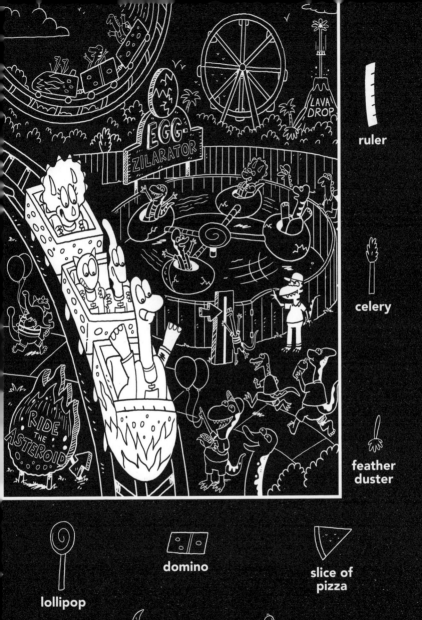

ruler

celery

feather duster

lollipop

domino

slice of pizza

crescent moon

bell

ice-cream
bar

ring

comb

baseball
bat

fried egg

golf club

fish

pencil

carrot

crescent
moon

hammer

toothbrush

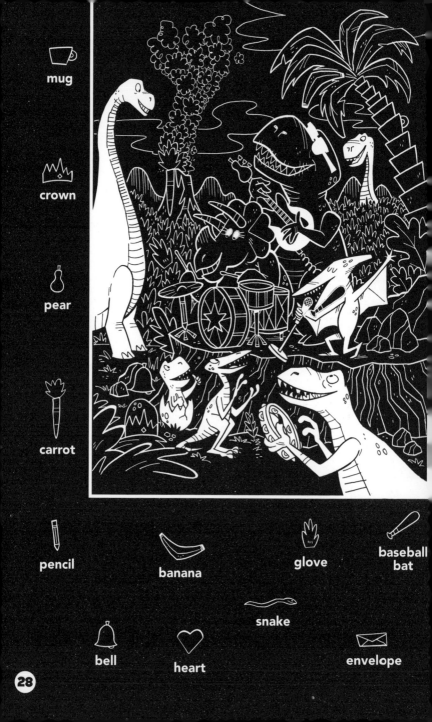

mug

crown

pear

carrot

pencil

banana

glove

baseball bat

snake

bell

heart

envelope

Page 4

Page 5

Page 6

Page 7

Page 14

Page 15

Pages 16–17

Page 18

Page 19

Pages 22–23

Page 24

Page 25